THE MOON
AS UNDERSTOOD
BY SKYSCRAPERS

THE MOON AS UNDERSTOOD BY SKYSCRAPERS

by Vinnie Sarrocco

CHATWIN BOOKS
SEATTLE, 2020

The Moon as Understood by Skyscrapers, by Vinnie Sarrocco

Text copyright Vinnie Sarrocco (Fiore Vincenzo Sarrocco), 2019-2020. Editorial & design copyright CHATWIN Books, 2020. Edited by Phil Bevis with the assistance of Helen Pendergast. Cover Design by Annie Brulé and Cyra Jane Hobson. Cover Illustration by Harry Reese. Book design by Annie Brulé. Interior layout by Cyra Jane Hobson. Author photo by Phil Bevis.

ISBN (paperback) 978-1-63398-112-6

www.chatwinbooks.com

Dedicated to Nicole

&

To every stranger in an unfamiliar city

CONTENTS

poems

I   9

II   35

III   57

acknowledgements   89

PORTRAIT OF A STOIC IN AUGUST

The sturgeon moon glowers down
at mortal shuffling behind windows,
on street corners, inside rib cages.
It climbs the sky leisurely
before swimming back inside itself.

Somewhere outside the walls
of my apartment a siren keens
for the city, which like the moon
has no more use for people.

Inside there is a waning
rocks glass dripping rings
of condensation onto an oak
coffee table in an empty room.

I've leaked teeth onto a pillow.
I've sweated out one thousand days of poison.
I've slept inside your ditch
and like the moon I've risen indifferent.

TALL TALES FOR SHORT PEOPLE

Those of us who were born
under a superstitious moon
cautioned by old wives' tales
or lulled to sleep with campfire folklore
carry that mythos in our bones
no amount of book learning
can change that, and really

what does it hurt
to hold your breath
when passing potter's fields
as I do

Let us spill new marrow
all over the asinine
so the children will have
novel songs to sing:
  like how splashing through the
murky sidewalk pools
will anger the water gods
and bring misfortune
to the person whose name was last
conjured in the steam of your breath
  like how surrendering your body
to jeans the next size up
will create space
for that beer-swollen paunch
to act as a liquid
and expand its shape even further
  like how if a moth mistakes

the light from your cell phone
for the immolation of a star
and gingerly lands on the screen
it is a sure sign that the burning
love possessing you is unrequited

Stories about the protective qualities
of Johnny's Seasoning Salt and Old Bay
the healing properties of lime and cantaloupe
how the size of one's hat
can affect the cut of one's jib
how to read the future
in the sound of a thunderclap

Speak these words
until they are meaningless cliches
masking intuitive truths
the way shamans
and baseball managers do

HIGHWAY EFFIGY

We crested a hill laden with oaks;
pallbearers ushering
our rattling Chevy coffin
towards an ocean
we planned to spread ourselves in.

We saw the smoke first
worming its way towards the firmament,
then the overturned semi—
axles exposed and pleading
for help.

No sign of a driver.
No sign of a heartbeat for miles.
No branding on the cab
or trailer, just bare corrugated metal
smoldering against the asphalt.

I thought of that Terry Allen song;
the truckload of art.
I thought of all the works
in the Met reduced
to glowing embers and ash.

I wanted to take it with us
where it was we were going.
I wanted to float alongside
a great tragedy.

INVENTORY OF AN AFTERNOON

An old woman and an old dog board the bus
together, they help each other into their seats.
They are tired of motion
tired of pace, tired of blood,
of shuffling through the veins of the city.
They are too tired to rest.
The dog smiles at me.
He is cursed
cursed with a mouth that can't close,
cursed with sincerity and callow joy,
his mournful howl misplaced somewhere terrible,
somewhere he used to eat and sleep
while waiting to be put down;
a place not dissimilar to the one the woman
eats and sleeps in now.
They only ride for one stop.

I get off later, at the park
where the well-bred dogs with mushy faces,
breathing problems and Instagram pages
sniff one another's asses.
It is a pleasant enough day.
The sun whispers life through a cloudless sky.
People are frolicking the way they only do
in poems and old silver-screen musicals.
They are a spate of spirit,
perpetual motion machines,
cold-fusion reactors, they have never once felt
tired.

There is a couple picnicking.
They are spread over a herringbone blanket.
The man pours a demi bottle of wine
into two styrofoam cups.
It feels unimaginably important
the way light catches his smile
like a fugitive underneath a helicopter at night.
The woman leans back, cradles
her weight in her palm.
I don't believe that she is happy.

I am merely passing through
on the way to a cave,
away from the barking
rays of sunshine;
a place that exists outside of time
where my acquaintances and I can be,
without anyone daring to be merry—
without anyone pining for a rest.

RUMINATIONS ON THE 10 MILLION DOLLAR FIST

Got to hand it to him
he's not lacking for moxie,
though maybe coherence,
but who hasn't at some point
felt betrayed by their government
and yearned for destruction
in the abstract?

Who hasn't been let down
by the impressionists in person?
Felt betrayed
by those blurry out-of-focus breasts—
antennae for the absinthe dreams
of Manet and Lautrec
or been taunted by the mocking serenity
of Monet's water lilies?

I must imagine the basin
with its single sailboat
was finally too much to bear.

Now there is a flash game
at punchmonet.com
where us regular folk can have our hands
painted in pixels and weaponized
against digital recreations of priceless art
and this is beautiful
far more so than any oil on canvas.

ODE TO THE GUY PRACTICING HARMONICA ON THE NUMBER 8 BUS DURING RUSH HOUR

O' to be a sardine;
inside an oily Goldberg abstraction,
or outside the canvas—
rattling down Denny Way,
crammed in a tremorous tin can
spitting diesel and mustard
at the pedestrians trapped
by overzealous commuters
reclined in the intersection.

O' to be a sardine;
nestled knees together, cheeks
straddling a torn vinyl saddle
mounted on a cannery conveyor belt
stained an unidentifiable color
by some unidentifiable substance.
Steeping in the putrid fish smell
and working class malaise that
climbs the walls in drab olive squiggles.

O' to be a sardine;
relegated to the bus lane headaches
and further, forced to endure the shrieking
reeds of an anguished French harp
fellated by a novice.
O' to be a sardine
with no vocal cords to use to scream:
"hey asshole,
quit blowing into that fucking thing!"

FOR THE ANNIVERSARY OF YOUR DEATH

A poet died today
an important one, I'm told:

The coffee table
        is still the same—
stained with character
        and my regrets
               and other's ideas.
The bum on First
        is still the same—
stained with character
        sleeping in front of the door
              indignant when asked to roll over.
The coffee is bitter—
        like the people
commuting to places
        they'd rather not
               have to be

The big difference,
as far as I can tell,
               is
W.S. Merwin's Amazon numbers
are absolutely off the charts.

CAUSATION

Time and time again
as consistently as cliches
arise in the diatribes
and esoteric laments
of charismatic men
or consistently as history
and Michael Bay repeat
their past iterations
bothering only to mask the farce
behind a thin veneer of glitz

we the denizens of consciousness
find ourselves being
so wholly burdened by being
anything at all
so at the mercy of our individual mercies and
so predisposed to be unmerciful
tangled in our own vile ouroboros
spewing venom at ourselves
then at each other
or vice versa
chicken egg
etc

I wane poetic
from inside a hammock's
netty embrace
Why not give yourselves a break
but the onlooking faces and sphincters
only tighten at the thought.

MARY

I'd like to mourn
the loss of her words;
the way she arranged them
so precise and delicate,
accessible, and not in *that* way,
not the pejorative the corduroy kids
and MFA grads use.

The Seattle sky is heavy
like the eyes of a child
who's been told crying
is reserved only for little girls.
The sky is swollen,
puffy and red
as even the sun retreats
to hide its face.

I too am pacified
ashamed and dissatisfied
paralyzed by indecision
ensconced in the stratosphere
but I do know
that I'd like to mourn.

MISSOURI CITY, KS

It's only powerful because we decide
it has that possibility

she decides that she will draw
boxes around anything

that slips into her peripheral
until she stares across a sea

of perfectly horizontal and vertical lines
intersecting one another

at seemingly asinine vertices—
a drunkenly composed graph

paper lined pair of sunglasses
that bounces off her

sun flushed cheeks at every bump
in every new road she meets

I tell her that we can be anywhere
any time we want

I tell her that we are going
to Missouri City, Kansas

I will tell her through lips pursed
into the most believable

of grins, the kind of smile
that can't be ignored

but should be at all cost, and later
hurtling across earth's

flattest strip of highway out of
one horizon and into another

I will look over my shoulder,
see the empty passenger seat

and realize my mistake

IGNORE THE WIZARD

Dorothy clacks her heels

against each other
        against herself:

there's no place
        there's no place

there is no space for her
        to physically occupy

                outside of her REM states

empty kettles and boiling points
        stovetop burners radiating

kitchen air foggy with sorrow
        and great plain tedium

whistling in the inner-ear
        all-encompassing tinnitus

                screaming through

righteous curtains
        ripe for burning

there's no place
        there's no place

to seek solace
        no trance or dream

            devoid of tin-men

pursuing cardiac rhythm
        beating chests instead
beating dead horses
        and straw-man fallacies

with bludgeons made
        from coward's bones

            there's no place to call home

no more country left to roam

there is screaming

to drown out regret

there is screaming

in all directions

there is an end to manifest destiny

the waves of two different oceans

crash into her

and she will swim

or she will float

or she will drown.

BREATHLESS PLATITUDES

A well-meaning teacher once told me:
aim for the moon, and if you fail
at least you'll be among the stars.

How vapid, I thought.
With the stars being beyond
the moon and what-not.

I would be marooned in un-inhabitable space
asphyxiating on ruptured lungs
until I popped like a cyst.

I took her advice anyway
and now spend my time trying to breathe
in the big city air.

A JESTER'S LAMENT

you only love me
when my chin touches my chest
and my boots chirp and squeal
on the concrete
as they drag their haggard corpse
from drink to drink

you only love me
when I sink into the well;
too listless to call for Lassie
enthralled by the mildew aroma
in my hair and spilling out my ears—
content in dampness

you only love me
when my stomach starts
to cannibalize itself
on a desert highway,
the growls echoing
the coyote's call

in these moments I am alive
pregnant with verve—
my ennui stretchmarked and ready to rupture
at the slightest crook of your lips
or at the sound
of a deadbolt latching

you only love me
when I am sad
or when I'm being funny;

these things being merely synonyms
you only love me
when I am sad
        and I too

LACHRYPHAGY

*Lachryphagy: The process by which some butterflies
and moths feed on the tears of other animals*

It is the sounds of feet fluttering—
ominous grace unnoticed by the man
facedown muttering through sleep
to the God of Those Who Listen.
His unholy memories manifesting
in the cavities of his teeth
and the part of the tongue
that puckers on lemon flesh.

They flutter closer
sensing the ripeness
with primordial instincts,
craving the saccharine sustenance
of heartaches and paroxysms.

The city is a pot of honey
in a Saturday morning cartoon
spilling nectar over its sides
into the suburbs;

It is the lamp everlasting.
Can you blame the moth?
The butterfly in all its anthropomorphized
friendship;
when its spiny legs tear
at his eyelids
and excavate anguish?
Can you blame those who flourish

in men's misery?

I'd like not to believe that
the buddleias weep for spring;
that those we most revere
find their life in another's loss,
but it becomes harder to deny
with every new cycle of the moon

GEMINI TOWN

> *A town needs a river to forgive the town.*
> —Richard Hugo

Up where the mighty Mississippi
draws its first inhalations of life
before dribbling down Sam's chin
we wade through humidity;
ambling lethargically against
the weight of moisture,
against the weight of sorrow
sometimes found in big city breezes.

The body of a young woman
rests crumpled underneath
a 19th century stone arched bridge,
dressed in a heroin nod and not much else;
she might be mistaken for dead
if not for the twitching spasms of life
fitfully depolarizing her neurons
like fresh fish meat in foil and lemon juice.

We are drunk on cheap whiskey
and the feeling of being somewhere
where you are a stranger.
We are inside the Mall of America
where excess is lauded
and large men vomit on log rides
splattering unsuspecting children
with french fries and Bud Light.

We are sailing a raft down the river.
We are a metaphor for everything
we wish could be undone.
We are the sounds of syllables
echoing across the pages
of a 200 year-old story, and
we are tired of waiting
for a happy ending.

MASQUERADE BALL

There is a beard:
wild, itching and
stained by turmeric
to the color of autumn.
It is a fig leaf,

I am 400 wasps
vibrating in a tight-knit
person-shaped mass then
adorned in denim and
gas station sunglasses.

I am in a place
where I used to dream.
The cicadas are there too,
their skeletons singing
among the wild oaks.

You are standing barefoot
with creekwater weeping
past your spiny legs.
You gracefully place
the molted remains

of chirping veils on an altar
made up of branch bones.
You have never once
recognized me. I am
thankful for this.

Everything is a mirror
if you're looking
to see yourself.
I live without
a reflection to shave by.

11

LOVE POEM

I like the burnt
edges of things
like toast, the
lacy ends of pastry
the cheese that drips off
of the burger
and sticks to the griddle
the stuff people carry
around on the tips
of their tongues
and in the backs
of their heads
the pieces of them
someone left carelessly
too close to the fire for
too long
I like the crunch
the bitter way it
sits in your mouth
and I'm instantly wary
of anyone who discards them

ROSES ARE VIOLENT

I'd like to write of fire
of passionate rams,
self-immolating monks,
burning away impurities
like a child's room
post scarlet fever;
stuffed bunny and all,
of amaryllis in bloom,
of manic vermillion eyes
bloodshot and seeking,
wine dark lips
pursed against bulletproof
plexiglass, phone dangling
dripping static
onto blood-stained concrete,

but I only have Carolina-blue
tinted cataracts,
an azure sky overhead
peeking through gaps
in the stratus clouds
swollen with murky
polluted acidic rain,
the cooling menthol
of melancholia—pervasive
and numbing,
the smell of lavender
clinging to my lush nose hairs;
the last pieces of a wild body
at rest, tamed by two oceans
for worse or for better—
ask me tomorrow

IMPOSTERS

He sits, hunched at the spine
tearing hairs from his cheek
with filth-filled fingernails
then dropping them in his drink
to see something float
and contrast his sinking
posture, his youthful hopes
deliquescing into a puddle
further poisoning the taupe
carpets, already stained with white ash
and the weight of impossible dreams

Who is he kidding?
the New York School is just Harvard
another unattainable station
like all stations
even the Greyhound these days
who has two hundred dollars?
Might as well be an answer
to a Big Question
The kind of answer people
who use the word ontology
pretend that they have

He sits, reading an anthology
The New-ish American
Poetry he oughta read
so as not to make the same mistakes
as those who have yet to come before
and check for themselves
in the scraps of sycamores

and while it makes no real difference
and he'll still be buried beneath
the pedantry of masters and academics
is there not something valiant
in the attempt, and isn't it
strange the way some men float
instead of limp?
isn't it strange the way some
men lean into their polemics
like a crutch?
Take me for example.

BEST COAST

The ramshackle wood
comprising the bar patio
all knotted and splintered
has become one with him
the rain and sweat soaked sleeping bag
a molecular adhesive
surgical glue
fusing man and the lesser matters
back together

Words ooze out horizontally
wispy syllables carried to the sky
by the heat of his breath
the sans serif typeface visible only
to those who pay attention
we're all in this together
I'm inclined to believe
him today

HOUTOUWAN VILLAGE (A NATURAL EKPHRASTIC)

We like to believe
in our permanence.
In lasting impact.
In ourselves and in
our worthiness
to be remembered;
we like to believe that
what we've assigned
so much capital *I*
Importance must hold
paramount in the fingers
and stomachs of those
who are ill-fated enough
to navigate this celestial boulder
post-you
because it simply has to.

Why else would we have
labored, sweat and bled,
deferred our lusts
and tabled the immediacy
of passion if we
were only building castles
out of sand
waiting for the tide
to reclaim what is
rightfully hers.

I walk through the moss
the living greenery

a rightful heir reinstalled.
I know it is all ephemera:
our written words, our language
itself, our buildings, our ideologies
and our romantic notions.

All like fleeting moments
of afterglow on a crisp
autumn morning
next to your lover
wrapped in a duvet
of time that forsakes
linear structure in favor
of a unique temporality
that blossoms for only
a moment, but somehow
lasts a lifetime.

MULLIGAN

And in that moment I was sure
I heard the clucking of chickens
returning home.
Did I consider myself an exception?
Did I expect a more dramatic
27 club bathtub nap
car crash overdose type exit?
Instead there is the highway
rolling by as my chest stiffens,
my fingers reject sensation,
extremities freeze for lack of life,
each heartbeat beats my breath
farther back in my throat.

The last decade spent in debauch
flashes across the median:
carousing across state lines
burning my body for fuel,
the damage done irreparable,
the question of worth inconsequential.
I make a deal without god
to put the bottle down,
throw away my ashtrays,
eat more kale and less human flesh.
I mean it.
I really mean it.
I wake up in the morning
I put on my boots.
I take three of the deepest breaths.
I feel fine.
I smoke on the way to work.

COUNTRY MUSIC

Johnny's wearing his bad luck
draped over his shoulders,
tied across his chest
like some waspy teenage
knuckle magnet.
It is a cloud following him
like in those old pencil-sketched
animated antidepressants ads
they used to show in the early aughts.
It flutters like a cape
as he walks from loss to loss
amassing debts that will be collected
on Tuesday nights at 11:11
when sleep is only a dream

I remember Burroughs telling
a class of young unbroken idealists
the only law he believed in
was the law of streaks.
It felt like he was talking to me
an internet-aided seance
summoning a loon or a prophet
into my teenage ear canal.
Watching Johnny waltz
across the warehouse with Miss Fortune
I'm inclined to believe Will was the latter.
But then I remember how
he mistook his wife's head for an apple,
and the former seems more probable.
I reckon snakebit recognize snakebit,
and you can't make antivenom
without poisoning another animal first.

SCULPTURE

Your panic left a scar
on my forearm
right above the inky fluttering
wings of teenage angst
I immortalized one clear
as moonshine summer night.
I drag fingertips across
the discolored skin sometimes
and feel the way you've changed
me structurally.
Then I wonder
if after Michelangelo
carved a brain into David
he immediately longed
to return to life as a stone.

GOING TO SHOWS ALONE

The air has been aged
in the musk of ten thousand
sweaty iconoclasts
bleeding intensity
onto painted concrete
sticky with spilled beer
spit and god knows what else
The opener wails on
scorned by the sound guy—
petulant noise for the
sake of forsaking silence.
I am the cheese
meandering between
bar and phalanx
of cross-armed hipsters;
a bona fide battalion
of lonely hearts
too old to wage war.
The headliner will arrive
like a second coming
the ecstasy of art
and religion not dissimilar.
I will leave tired
ears suffused with feedback.
I will leave thinking
it was almost worth it.

FLIGHT OF THE BOUNCY HOUSE

The children gather
to spit in gravities face
and chortle at humanities
physical limitations that
way only young people can—
all hubris unburdened
by a life, and its failures
so they bounce with nothing
to weigh them down
land and bounce higher
then
suddenly
too high
and the comfort of the Earth's
crust shrinks like a wool sweater
in a hot dryer
and their bodies float away
to be reclaimed
by the cosmos.

FENG SHUI

I want to live in a 7/11
parking lot somewhere
outside of Memphis
I want to sharpen my irises
against the glares of frenzied
men with nothing to lose
except a few more teeth
I want to recline
under the leery watch
of a young clerk who's been
robbed too many times
his hands caressing
a Louisville Slugger
while he contemplates
his future—deciding if a future
is even what he wants
I want to taste the regret
the way it tricks the tongue
into mistaking its metallic tang
for a mouthful of earnestness
I want to awaken alert out of necessity
I want the immediacy of fear and
I want there to be no question
I am alive

RUBY MOODS

She is a poinsettia in spring
her back bowed
shoulders slouched
knees drawn high
in fetal elegance
her toxic leaves wilting
underneath April's glimmering countenance
a tepid reminder of bygone revelry
fruitcake and fighting
your blood across plastic card tables
while a dying conifer drips needles
and illuminates the living room
she is an anachronism
a memento of a good time
that only exists in retrospect
and optimistic premonitions
she is trying
her best

INSOMNIA

Haunted by the ghosts
of people you used to be
of ideas you once entertained
sounds that slipped past your cracked lips
and spilled out onto the rug
oh, the one nice thing she owned
ruined—stained with your breath
there is no scotchgard for language
you swallow it down
between glasses of Dewars
swimming in it until
your eyes burn and redden
your ears fill with the fermented crop
muting the chain rattle
coming from the bedsheets and walk-in closet
pleading for your attention
the petulant child inside your ribs
wails because there is simply
no alternative to wailing
those impotent cries reminiscent
of the manic drug induced music
of your early years
wraiths accumulate on stage
tapping djembes and twisting
the knobs of synthesizers
dancing and laughing
until tears stream down their spectral face
until nobody remembers what it was
they were feeling
in the first place

REGULARS

It's something like Cheers
only older and angrier
and one of them dies off
every mid-season arc
the rest of the cast remembers
and drinks to remember
and the tontine pot
grows and swells
like a tampon
dipped in clamato juice
then one day the lead
rolls in saddling a mobility scooter
and the youngest one of the bunch
has a liver with too much quit
and he grows and swells
like a tampon
dipped in clamato juice
and I laugh, red-faced
at their jokes and
fights and the wood stain
chips off the ancient bar
and the copper taps rust
and I laugh, red-faced
into the clairvoyant's
crystal ball
at all the mistakes
I've yet to make

THE LAST MAN ON EARTH STILL WAITING TO BE CRUSHED BY A PIECE OF SKYLAB

He wakes up cold
naked, neck kinked
from staring down
the stars. He's
drenched in sweat—
the salt rejected
by a body
stains jersey sheets
and a yellowed twin-size mattress—
found not purchased years ago
in another city, another lifetime,
one before the visions
of fiery metal plummeting
towards his unsuspecting skull
fluttered like Super-8
footage being projected
against heavy islands of eyelids.

He checks the ceiling for holes.
He approaches the window
gazes below in search of concrete
and devastation, singed tree tops
and sidewalk turned charred quarry
but finds only B-roll footage
of extras pretending to live
naturally between bus stops
and coffee shops.
He is disappointed.

Outside the sun beats against
a withered city.
He carries an umbrella anyway
hurries towards the corner store
glancing nervously upwards at
the planes sailing overhead.
It is worse inside.
He buys a newspaper, a cup of noodles,
and a box of wine
flees in a panic
shouting the whole way
back to his apartment.

The printing ink makes words
the words make sentences
but nowhere does he find
vindication for Chicken Little
and so sleep will again
have to be fought for.
If only he'd never turned on
the television back in '79.
If only the scientists at NASA
thought to tame their hubris
rather than the heavens.
If only he'd never grown
a pair of legs to crawl
out of the primordial soup with.
If only it would hurry up
and flatten him beneath
the weight of innovation
so he could simply
quit worrying about it.

SELF-PORTRAIT

Something about the way
Kokoshka signs his name
OK even though
he's clearly not
or the sight of a discarded
Vanity Fair underneath the stairs
to the alley with the dumpster
your own face
on the cover a
pentimento hidden by
Demi Moore's soon
to be born
or the selfies you post
of an uncanny doppelganger
whose lips almost
resemble the way I remember
they felt against my fingertips
back when we discovered
a tactile shorthand for skin

ICONTACT

We are walking
against the sun
and towards it
I look at her
as we step heel-toe
across a tightrope
neither of us
has time to notice
wobble underfoot
I look at her
like we could fall
in love at any
moment and later
full of whiskey
and misunderstandings
I'll step outside
nose to nose
with an offended party
frothing and shouting
and coming for my teeth
we'll beat our chests
circle each other and
I'll look at him
the same way

III

BAD OMEN

Perched on the cliff
overlooking the sound
she says she'd like to
be born again
an albatross
soaring above seas
too rough to sail
dancing web-footed and lustful
in island nests
that remain unblemished
by human ambition
to absorb the wisdom
of the pilot's vantage
to mate for life
and die
a righteous martyr
strung like christmas lights
across a salty neck
condemning man for his hubris

perched on the cliff
overlooking the sound
she turns
and smiles
at me

MY FRIEND

Teeth have been spilled
all over the yard—
yellowed enamel taking refuge
behind untrimmed weeds
like soldiers in a foreign land

He's suffering down there
in that city Sherman set ablaze.
I pray his reconstruction
will go smoother
than the South's.

It's all gums up here.
It's all tight lip smiles and novacaine
applesauce and feckless
neutered mountain lions

The grey dreadlocks he
left behind have been misplaced
it's not for me to find them
but I can't help seeking
them in every cafe

and poem I stumble upon.

WASTED

There is urgency in regret.
Those fleeting pieces
of present so petulant
when abandoned to the past—

    how they howl

        like a pack of wolf pups.

Today she is the moon
grey and scarred with impact

    craters.

    Yesterday she was

the wistful eyes
of a longshoreman
watching boats depart
to places he'll never go.

    The day before;

a lone sneaker deserted
in the street, tumbling
underneath tires, spinning
towards someone else's horizon.

    Tomorrow has yet to be

    decided

but if you made an educated guess
you would probably be right.

    It's funny like that—

how often we are our own
teleprompters scripting in real time,

and it's funny how
we can't see the now
until it's been
reshaped into a then.

    Come here.

Shed no more tears
for seconds lost
lest you find yourself
missing minutes.

    Come here.

    Laugh with me

and watch all our wasted time roll by
like the background in a black and white cartoon—
the ones they used to show
before the feature.

CYNICAL IN SEATTLE

It's really my fault
for wanting to see
something authentic
on a Tuesday
in this city
where even the rain acts
aloof, leaking from the
troposphere, misting
your eyes, but not quite
committed to falling.

It's really my fault
for not looking
hard enough.

THE REDNECK INVASION OF CARNEGIE HALL

The Carolina boys' hootin' an hollerin'
echos between ornate columns
older than their sins
and the sins of their fathers
drawing leers and ire
from the legacy class
those who are supposed
to be there
those who were bred for it
like swine born to be bathed in vinegar
dressed in coleslaw
and turned into BBQ sandwiches

Shit boy
one hollers
Is he's singing in German?
and they buck in their chairs
like wounded mares and
thank god there's no bottles to throw
or 18th century heirloom urns
to pool with dip spit
like the perennial pots after a morning dew

Must have greased themselves
with corn liquor and slipped
through the cracks in the ancient bricks
like thrice sprayed
pesticide resistant termites
littering 57th Street

with square body Chevys
and toothy sordid grins

Must be a reason
somewhere up there

SUBLUNARY PARADIGMS

On the night of the total
Lunar Eclipse
underneath the old penny
floats a barge
or maybe it's a yacht
dreamily anchored in the bay
filled with witnesses
to the celestial shadow theatre

its maritime glow
reminiscent of the Jeep 4 x 4s
with DIY lift kits
and LED light bars
the yokels would mount
as they wreaked havoc
on the countryside

I suppose
we're mostly the same and
there isn't large
climactic tectonic altering
change

like you find in movies

in the end
as predictably as the moon
moves through its phases
we conquer terrain
we smile and
combust

just because

MANHATTAN: WEEKDAY MORNING

Stories stacked like a ladder to heaven
rung after rung of homogenized cubicles
break room microwaves and the sort of ambition
that perpetuates itself for the sake of time already spent

Must be some kind of work going on
underneath those thousands of artificial suns
glimmering against the muted grey skyline boundless
in its pursuit to grab hold of the firmament and tame it

to drag the heavens down to eye level
and rub the Incomprehensible's face into the subway
  grating
until the trains push the hot garbage-scented smoke out
  in a wheeze

Must be some kind of work going on
underneath those thousands of dying stars
but you wouldn't know it just by looking out

your window,
and into theirs.

I've never been prouder to be.

PSALM FOR THE MAN LISTENING TO SOUL IN THE BALLARD PUBLIC LIBRARY'S RESTROOM

The soothsayer sits on his porcelain cathedra;
the hymns of Lee Moses blare out,
reverberating off stall dividers like an eldritch om—
an incantation to summon Bad Girls and Staple Singers
to this very lavatory I've slinked into
looking to wet my tongue with whiskey
away from the disapproving gaze of librarians
and people claiming to be poets.

The prophet plays on in a trance, disregarding any other
　bodies
that may occupy the room and the sounds of muted
off-key trumpets harmonize with the sounds of funk
　flushing—
blue notes sinking and careening into an already
overtaxed Seattle sewer system
until they re-emerge howling in full stereo
from the toilets of posh uptown apartments
occupied by tech bros and finance dorks

who desperately need some soul administered rectally.

MOTIVATIONAL

He is hunched
golf shirt stained
with coffee and quips
stolen from self-help sections
of suburban Barnes & Nobles.

His pockmarked skin
glistens with sweat
as he cooks beneath
industrial halogen lighting
like a naked cornish hen.

He turns on a video
featuring the charismatic
capitalist he'd like to be
Jeff Musk Gates or someone
pacing a stage

chin grown a microphone
biohacked / evolved
past divine rights
of kings
this is man's will
or so it seems.

Now for a powerpoint;
language but an obstacle
for him to stumble over—
a midwestern boomer's
grasp on technology
mitigates nothing.

I can't stop chuckling
at his overuse of the word penetrate.
Childish, I know
but scanning the room
there is not a shred of irony to be found
in the eyes of his employees

and I refuse to let the seriousness
of this display
remain unquestioned.

THE 1561 CELESTIAL PHENOMENON OVER NUREMBERG AND ITS MODERN APPLICATIONS

There has always been magic in light
in the sun and in the mother.
The mythos our collective minds have conjured
to make sense of enigmatic unrealities
and the incomprehensible experience of consciousness
since splitting into bicameral gray matter
may now be referred to as science
rather than magic in the vernacular;
it may be tested and peer-reviewed,
it may blanket us with comfort and
abdicate our dread curiosity and imagination
but modern folks might imagine the mass consternation
and awe such a sight as those lights
over Nuremberg inspired in middle man.
I sure can.

You see I was riding the bus the other day
when a cacophony of modem noises and emergency
  alerts
erupted from the pockets
of a hundred commuters simultaneously.
Heads dropped and hands dug into
purses like the first attempt at a synchronized
swimming routine—clumsily deliberate.
In that moment we were united by interruption,
unified by the unexpected and our fear
of the unexplainable.

We were ignorant peasants—
the dirty denizens of reformation-era Nuremberg
looking at our light and back at each other
in wonder.
      It was the most connected
I've ever felt to my community.

EGRESS

the air here sticks to you
ghosts haunt the humidity
they hold your head in the mud
singe your neck hairs
with scintillating radiation
born in distant stars
beyond the Milky Way
beyond even the Atlantic Ocean

the rivers here are at all times
flowing with four generations of blood
the deltas primed to swallow
unsuspecting young
ensnaring them in sediment
ensuring sustained spectral vitality

I've seen it
still

I return here
every so often
to bury the ones I left behind
but each visit becomes increasingly dangerous
the spirits are heavier now
or perhaps my knees
are beginning to buckle
under the weight of time
wraiths imbue me with visions
of past reveries and affordable housing markets
soon I begin to confuse malevolence
with quaint small town charm

and nearly succumb to the phantasmal thrall
this is just to say
I won't make it
to the next procession

OPPY

It gets lonely here sometimes
I get lonely and kick rocks
across Ares' pockmarked visage
as if Sisyphus
and imagine I am happy

What a burden it is
to outlive God's expectations
and how sluggishly ninety days
has mutated into fifteen years
though closer to seven up here

an eternity of solitary sensations
especially since the sand
snared my twin Spirit
like Zeus splitting man
it gets lonely here sometimes

and there are no more
birthday songs no more
rocks left unkicked
just the infinite dust
for me to chart

but

my battery is low
and it is getting dark

VOYAGER GOLDEN RECORDS

I am having trouble with hope
deciding whether it is more -less or -ful

with regards to humanity's
instincts to preserve
to bottle ourselves
in a rocket-propelled probe
now floating placidly across
an interstellar ocean
warm cosmic radiation
like piss in a Key West hotel's lazy river

the -ful for our desire to communicate
the -less for its dire necessity

I am a strong proponent of context
however
I hope there is none
should those records
ever spin to life and spew us
onto some unsuspecting alien race
I would prefer them not to know
what we were like
to each other
and to everything

When the Budapest String Quartet
finishes its cavatina
I would like them to think

we were beautiful
    because we could be
        not because we had to be

CARICATURE AT BEST

I feel it unfair
to pen hearts around
your mighty oaks when
the names of so many
cousins are already embossed
into the bark of hundreds
of gnarled branches.

Who am I now
to sing the murder ballads
and half-remembered banjo tunes
that were plucked
clawhammer style on my veins,
behind my eyes and on
your back porch.

This prodigal son
will return only when
it's convenient—a deadbeat
child with a Soviet memory
who abandoned home
instead of staying to fix it
stealing a gunny sack

of quips and synecdoches
on his way up
to whip out whenever
his patchwork personality
won't split wood.

Still, how could I
possibly ignore it?

How could I possibly
forget?

APOCALYPTIC VISIONS OF MR. CLEAN

My hairline hitches a ride with the teeth of my comb
like an expat with mystic country wisdom;
abandoning home
before the corruption that inundates
my face's greater metropolitan area
snakes up into the wooded northern mountains.

My body has been violently spun in an elongated oval
around the cosmos at roughly 67,000 miles per hour
no more than 25 times, and yet my hair
has already decided that 25 is too many
and seeks the comfort of bathroom tile
and the sustenance provided by damp porcelain sinks.

My targeted network of advertisements
assures me that this can be remedied with pills
and solvents and mostly easy monthly payments,
but I know there is a war of information happening;
I've found microscopic copies of Stirner's works
scrawled in tiny English onto my dandruff

My follicles are forsaking their community
in a misguided attempt to serve their individual
interests, and refuse to listen when I explain
they will only succeed in being swept up
with the dust and discarded into the garbage.
Perhaps they can't see past the scissors.

I've taken to saving my voice lately,
and wearing hats.

LIKE THE PORTRAITS OF EGON SCHIELE

You are harsh lines etched in canvas.

You are all bones and angles
twisted into angry knots,
tits, pubic hair and coiled
coy smiles.

You are half-shut eyes glaring into
the sun, only today is overcast
and tomorrow it will
be raining.

You are a jaw clenched tight enough
to tense the muscle fibers
down your calves, curling
your toes.

You are writhing manic motion—
an accidental contortionist.
A deranged Austrian
street performer

who gathers no audience
or schillings, just
empty tins and hurried
side-eyed glances.

You are squirming, wiggling,
you are jerking

for lack of air
you are

floundering through subsistence
like a timeless work of art.

TURTLE SOUP

You can withdraw behind ramparts,
cower beneath keratin
while the weight of 25,000 days
shifts uncomfortably on top your shell—
won't make you any less meat,
blood and substance. It
won't bulwark your spirit;
it's spirit all the way down you know.

Don't get me wrong, I get the impulse.
I too feel the pressure of mundanity—
the way it straddles your body,
licks its fingers before sticking them in your ears.

I know the way exhaustion builds
behind your eyelids while you lie
in between bed sheets begging simultaneously
for more time and less of it.

But what are you going to do?
Wait it out? Bee-line towards the sea?
Rock fetal until you've smoothed
yourself into a play-doh ball?

Truth is you're getting boiled
one way or another.

GONE THE WAY OF RAZORS

underneath the flickering
fluorescent glow of mercury;
the humming ode to failure—
capitalism's banal festival light show

our man stealing batteries—
a shrine to authenticity, I suppose,
or resilience of the human spirit
or maybe he's less shrine

more mirror
held by a vain
collection of ideas
in love with its dirtiest bits

or some Nottingham outlaw
to be lauded
the subject of odes
more inspired than this one

regardless,

the batteries live now
inside a glass panopticon
only the teenage bagboy
has the key to

a somber presage of our man's future

THE MAN INSIDE MY WALLS

only makes his presence known
when the moon presides over the morning
when the neighbors have all fallen into themselves
when our bodies lie the closest
and our minds are incongruous hermits
reveling in the kind of solipsism
that can only be understood in the dark

he hammers on the drywall
the couple downstairs complains about the noise
but the men on the phone are unable to listen
when the police come around
asking questions—searching for ghosts
wearing their impatience like stigmata
I will have nothing to say to them

there are plenty of tomorrows left to wait for

HOME

It's made of gypsum board and sadism
metal pipes carry lactic acid
between hermit crab shells
there are four eyes and
ears everywhere listening
collecting your syllables
turning them into safety pins
it will leave protruding from your pillows
it is never still
there are doors where once
there were windows
and vice versa
a long time ago
while you were sleeping
it carved you and crawled
into the cavity in your chest
where the bass should be
and left something else there
a round nothing sized something
you can feel your blood beat against
on the days when the mirrors are all fogged
and it rains inside

there is no place
like this

ANOTHER

I don't know these men
or the buildings they live in
all cheap pastel cement siding
and regurgitated aesthetics harking
back to a time that only existed
in a dimension obfuscated by hearts.
Were they ever children
or were they spit from the dirt
whole, already fitted into
their casings: maroon denim,
asymmetrical prints on short-sleeve
button-ups, meticulously coiffed,
dead-eyed and demure pressing
buttons creating light where there
should be none, desperately looking
for new rules to follow.
Perhaps they are still children
Perhaps I'm misremembering childhood
as grass stains and broken fingers
when it was more overhead lighting
and parsley tears.

It is overcast in the city
and will be
for the foreseeable future.

DEAD AIR

Traffic today moves like breath
inside a hospice house;
torpid sporadic swelling
and waning — effort
in every inch.

From the window I watch
seaplanes land on the lake,
cast shadows on the Olympics,
transcend the heaviness of spirit.
Oh, how I'd like to fly:

to float weightlessly
towards the thermosphere
in consonance with
the warm summer breeze.
Oh, how I'd like to fly.

Oh, how I'd like
to have somewhere
worth flying to.

ACKNOWLEDGEMENTS

Special thanks to Phil Bevis and Annie Brulé for all the hard work they put into creating such beautiful books.

Big thanks to Helen Pendergast for helping edit these words into some semblance of coherency.

Thanks and love to Rebecca Huvard for holding it down.

Thanks and love to Gena and Jim Jones for keeping Raleigh safe for me while I've been away.

Thanks to the Hugo House for providing a space for these poems to be read aloud and workshopped to death. The building is a constant source of inspiration.

Special thanks to the poets Erika Brumett, Tige DeCoster, Peter Munro, Heidi Seaborn, Paula Brentlinger, Peter O'Donovan, Lillo Way, Mark Johnson, Joan Perkins, and Holly Boone

Thanks to the editors of the following publications where a few of these poems have appeared in previous forms:

>*Cirque: A literary Journal for Alaska and the Pacifc Northwest*: "Regulars"
>*Duck Lake Journal:* "Tall Tales for Short People"
>*Rumble Fish Quarterly:* "Bad Omen"
>*The Poetry Box:* "Voyager Golden Records"
>*SPREAD:* "Best Coast, Egress"

VINNIE SARROCCO

Vinnie Sarrocco is a poet and raconteur from rural North Carolina. He currently works out of Seattle Washington, where he lives and masquerades as an upstanding citizen.

His work has been featured in *Cirque, Coffin Bell, The Poetry Box, Rue Scribe, Rumble Fish Quarterly,* & others. He is the author of the full-length collection *Poems for the Garbage Man* (Chatwin Books 2019).

www.ingramcontent.com/pod-product-compliance
Lightning Source LLC
Chambersburg PA
CBHW020442090526
44586CB00045B/786